OTHER TITLES FROM THE EMMA PRESS

POETRY ANTHOLOGIES

In Transit: Poems of Travel
Second Place Rosette: Poems about Britain
Everything That Can Happen: Poems about the Future
The Emma Press Anthology of Contemporary Gothic Verse

BOOKS FOR CHILDREN

When It Rains, by Rassi Narika
Dragons of the Prime: Poems about Dinosaurs
Super Guppy, by Edward van de Vendel
Poems the wind blew in, by Karmelo C Iribarren

PROSE PAMPHLETS

First fox, by Leanne Radojkovich
The Secret Box, by Daina Tabūna
Tiny Moons, by Nina Mingya Powles
Postcard Stories 2, by Jan Carson

POETRY PAMPHLETS

The Stack Of Owls Is Getting Higher, by Dawn Watson
A warm and snouting thing, by Ramona Herdman
The Whimsy of Dank Ju-Ju, by Sascha Aurora Akhtar
Vivarium, by Maarja Pärtna

THE EMMA PRESS PICKS

Birmingham Jazz Incarnation, by Simon Turner
Bezdelki, by Carol Rumens
Requiem, by Síofra McSherry
Call and Response, by Rachel Spence

THE EMMA PRESS

ANTHOLOGY
OF ILLNESS

Edited by Amy Mackelden
and Dr Dylan Jaggard

THE EMMA PRESS

First published in the UK in 2020 by the Emma Press Ltd

ISBN 978-1-910139-53-0

A CIP catalogue record of this book
is available from the British Library.

Printed and bound in the UK by Imprint Digital, Exeter.

The Emma Press
theemmapress.com
hello@theemmapress.com
Jewellery Quarter, Birmingham, UK

INTRODUCTION

Painfully often, disabled people are spoken over, misrepresented, or forgotten altogether, which is why we cannot speak on behalf of the voices contained in this volume. But we can attempt to drive home one essential fact: disabled and chronically sick people are people.

Television and movies might tie our lives up in convenient bows and suggest that there's nothing worse than illness, but – as anyone who has grappled with a condition knows – life goes on, even when it's hard and we've low-key prayed to Tom Cruise to relieve our suffering on multiple occasions. A person's worth isn't measured like the battery percentage on a smartphone, and, as these poems attest, life gets messy and can seem unworkable, but that's okay.

From interactions with devastatingly sexy medics to drastic miscommunications to prolonged symptoms without answers, the poets in this anthology have laid their nervous systems bare, lesions and all. People talk of finding a "new normal" after a health scare, and that can be true, sure. But these poems explore the purgatory of illness, and the unexpected swerves a life can take while waiting for a doctor's lips to move.

We, too, have received diagnoses that have reduced us to the consistency of blancmange. Between us, we've done therapy, been admitted to psychiatric facilities, undergone disease-modifying treatments which carried the threat of progressive multifocal leukoencephalopathy, had our faulty ovaries examined, attended self-harm club, trialled a slew of antidepressants, and genuinely wondered whether our lives would continue. Spoiler alert: they did.

We could only include a small selection of the work we received, but we're beyond grateful for everyone's honesty. Thank you all for opening up a dialogue about what it means to be sick AF.

Amy Mackelden and Dr Dylan Jaggard
MAY 2020

CONTENTS

ଔ

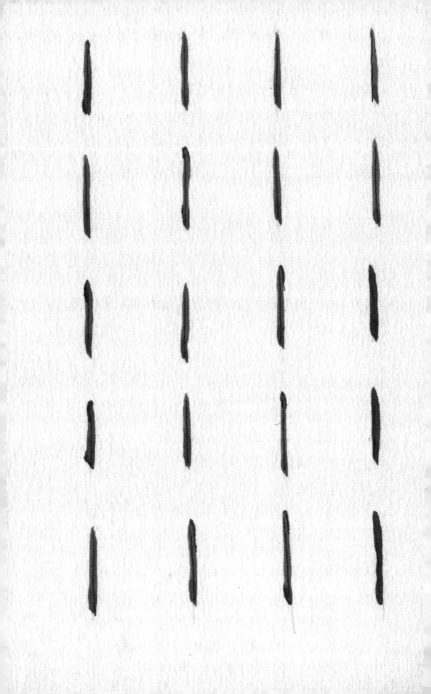

Terms and Conditions

Welcome to Chronic Illness.

With Chronic Illness, you can have all the perks
that you have ever wished for, with a few
small
sacrifices.

Terms and Conditions will apply to your conditions –
please read them cautiously.

Please note: Chronic Illness is a lifelong
commitment and it is extremely difficult to revert
once you have developed your illness(es).

1:
You are permitted an extra 30 minutes
in bed, every morning.*

   ** No sleep or rest is included in this plan, and
you are required to be in excruciating pain
for the duration of your stay.*

2:
Reduced social interaction with strangers.*

   ** This occurs on the basis that they whisper
about you right in front of you, and pretend that
you do not exist.*

3:

Increased personal space.*

This occurs with the public being under the impression that you are diseased and they do not want to catch your illness(es).

4:

You will not look sick, disabled or ill.*

This will result in comments such as 'I've felt like that before', or 'Why don't you try this remedy?'

5:

You are permitted to leave social gatherings early, or cancel them altogether.*

Decreased mental status may occur due to the embarrassment. Pain will increase during the time it takes to explain your condition(s) to the other parties, who still may not understand.

Side effects of Chronic Illness may include:
    severe stomach cramps
    stabbing pains in lungs
    frequent headaches and migraine
Symptoms will vary from person to person.

Please monitor your own body closely to understand all personal side effects of Chronic Illness.

Further symptoms may arise if medication is taken.

Please consult your doctor if any abnormal or worrying symptoms occur.

The Problem with Good-Looking Oncologists

His eyes are blue and butterfly
across the scan. I slip off my cardigan,
my T-shirt, *Shall I..?* He nods, all Bryan Adams
stubble and unwoken hair, pressing
the image onto the lightbox
as I unclasp my bra, fold it cup into cup and
lay it on the chair, my stomach fluttering.
I will my nipples to behave
as I lie down, distract myself with
a painting of a flower, its veined petals brimming
round a yellow stamen. He swivels
towards me and they harden like winkles.
You all right? He glances down, a quick neat smile,
then back to the screen where
my breast's lit up, a photo negative of a fritillary wing,
the patterns contracting and expanding at his touch,
each duct hopeful and glittering:
Pick me! Pick me!

Binge

she gulps peach slices and   tinned pears
cured meats and   memories   preserved in brine
      she gulps Jaffa Cakes
  and slabs of processed   solitude

she is in a lavatory
in a cold room
on her lunch break
at six minutes past one

she does it quietly, steadily
because no-one's told her to
because it weighs her like ballast
because it fits like a straitjacket

it tastes of   habit,
      of   sugared almonds,
      of   sleeping pills
  and warm milk

      of something that once flowed abundantly
but she kept to herself
like a fresh cut.

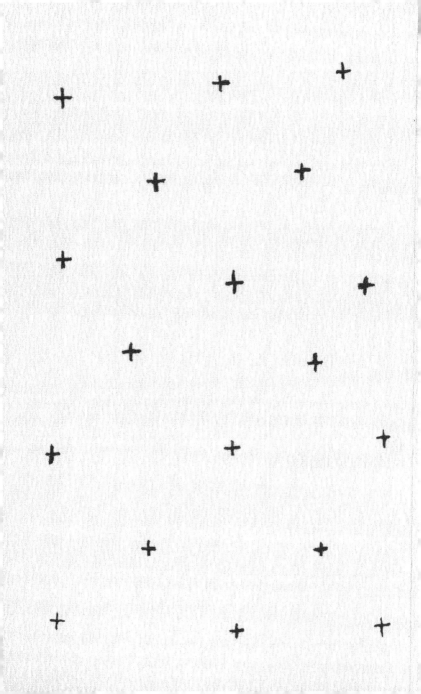

Kissing Disease

The summer we sat our O-Levels
we went to Pontins to practise kissing,
me and my best friend Maxine.
She had blue-black hair, flashing eyes,
and within a day was crowned Miss Bay View.

My consolation prize was a throat
as cracked as an old satchel and a set
of gobstopper glands. My kiss-me-quick
hat perched on the edge of my fevered bed,
eyeing me as I tossed and turned,
sweated puppy fat by the pound.

Meanwhile Maxine dazzled
a Bluecoat, lured him back to the chalet
where they fumbled and groaned
in the fusty gloom. I covered my head
with the brushed nylon sheet and fumed.
Now and then, she smuggled a pot
of jelly from the café: a lava-red
slow slip down my ungrateful gullet.
By the fifth night, as she curled her hair,
hummed along to *summer lovin'* on the radio,
I flipped: *Call yourself a fockin' friend?*
How dare you go out without me?

After, when my dad dropped her off,
we exchanged a secret, shameful look.
The next year we went to Lanzarote.
Me and my best friend Julie.

Mees' Lines

It takes a year for the four white stripes on my nails to grow out. Evenly-spaced transverse bands of white discolouration on my nail plate, I'm told I should think of them as my growth rings, my tree rings. But I bite them to the quick and cover them with nail polish, from cuticle to tip. When you take my hand, I curl my fingers around yours, hiding the ridges. Later, I push back my cuticle to examine my lunula for chalky striations, but I find only a waning gibbous.

The Cutter's Tale

Each night it surrounds you –
something sinking comes to ruin
the good parts of the day and turn
your femininity sour, reminding you

the harmful words you spewed
at day's end would return –
things you said when burned
by condescending men. Now too

unsexed in the mirror, you want to join
in bullying's booming industry
yet feel inferior for giving them hell,

tying the score through portioned pain
illicit on your skin (ire's artistry),
cutting with razor strokes that always heal.

Fibroid Haiku

paper knickers on
    myomectomy today
        frail hope stings sore eyes

Cross-Section with Contrast

They are picturing the inside of my body:
abdominal cavity, blood vessels, bones.
Iodine pulses through my veins, flushes warm
and wet between my legs. I've been forewarned,
assured I will not piss myself. A man with kind eyes
squeezes my hand, twice, then steps behind a screen.
I wonder if it's bulletproof? I'm on my back, stripped
of my wedding ring, the necklace from my daughters.
They hold no traction here, in this room of machines
that ignore the heart in favour of the stiller organs.

Cones

When I tell you I'm mad
  as a March hare,
  as a box of frogs,
  as a man shaking a dead geranium,
you will plonk me, lickety-split into
a jar, screw down the lid,
look for a label.
Your raised brow will circle me,
inspect my slug's foot splayed
up against the inside.

When I tell you I'm mad,
  away with the fairies,
  lost in space,
  howling at the moon,
your thoughts will shift from foot
to foot, glimpse at their watches.

When I tell you I'm mad,
  loopy,
  doolally,
  deranged,
you will say I am
  brave
to tell you,
and place yellow plastic cones around me.

When I tell you I'm mad,
bonkers,
brainsick,
bananas,
you will find yourself glued
to a night road, eyes wide, nose twitching
and I'll be full-beaming towards you,
fumbling
for the off switch.

I am a pantheist and don't believe in god, but there have been moments when I've prayed to some people's Imaginary Sky Friend

on some of the nights (and days) when I would hunch on the toilet seat

for twenty

thirty

forty

minutes at a time,

over a toilet bowl filled with blood and shit and waiting for more to come out of me

because this had been the life I'd lived for years and this is what I knew –

blood and shit and pain;

on some of those nights (and days) when I was tired of bleeding,

tired of being afraid of food, tired of my life,

I would look up at the dusty lightbulb and cry and tell god that if he made it go away

then I promised I'd believe in him

but it never went away and so I didn't believe

on some of the nights when I would huddle in a ball in the corner of my bed

with my back wracked with spasms and my belly playing host

to a stampede of frightened elephants who were trampling over my intestines,
my shirt clinging to my skin from sweat and pain;
on some of those nights when I was just so tired,
so very very tired of interrupted sleep and pain and medications and having people stick
  things in my body
and never being able to escape any of it,
of waking up every morning to know there is more of the same ahead,
I would look out into the darkness around me and cry and tell god that if he made it go away
then I promised I'd believe in him

but it never went away and so I didn't believe

on the nights when I lay there waiting for a surgeon's knife to cut into me
lying wrapped in a pale blue gown, attached to machines that blinked and beeped and
drew jagged lines that traced my life
I would close my eyes and cry and tell god that if he let me die, if he let me escape my body
then I promised I'd believe in him

but I didn't go away and so I don't believe

15

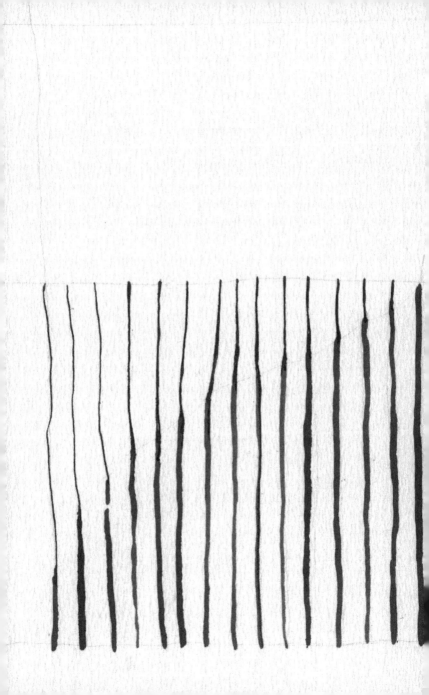

My Nephew's Second Birthday: A Saga of Self-Stimulatory Behaviour

In three out five.

'Remember to breathe,' says the woman I've never met,
as if I could forget, as if her child's party bag had come to life
and wrapped itself around my neck.

In three out five.

My sister had dutifully planned the seating arrangement:
his family on the left, ours the right. The placard that delegates my space
rests on the lid of the toilet seat, where I spend most of my evening,
avoiding discordant symphonies of children screaming,
bootleg covers of disco hits and phones keening like tinnitus.

In three out five.

I am a balloon dressed in black: not in the party mood.
Primary pain sears my eyes and plays musical bumps behind the lids,
higher and higher helium sounds stretching my eardrums and skin so thin I'm ready to burst

In three out five.

into tears. I cannot be the only one crying at a toddler's birthday party.
If I do it over the cake, parents will smoke like party poppers,
the coloured confetti falling out in questions. My relatives will explain,
embarrassed, ashamed, she can't help it, she just gets like this sometimes,
born with a faulty aux cable to her brain, the manual was in Swedish, unknown European make,

In three out five.

I am foreign flat-packed furniture: frustrating,
when my hands start shaking and my spine starts swaying,
a broken cubicle door, creaking and crying an SOS: Sensory Overload Sucks,

18

In three out five.

I am not broken. My bones just need more oiling.

A specialist technician knows exactly where my wires are going.

The neurodivergent can keep going and going, faster and further than some standard models; they just overheat sooner, need more time on battery saver.

Let me let out some air, allow my rubber skin to sag, and stim, even if it means I'm floating lower today.

In three out five.

I remember to breathe, no longer having to regulate it manually.

Outside the quiet bathroom sanctuary, the party continues without me.

The candles go out in a single breath, five seconds, no less.

High Dependency Unit

Frank screams every time they move him:
his cracked hips pierce each quarter hour.

I am blind to his trouble,
curtained from my neighbours:

the fallen ones, the sepsis cases –
it's best to keep the worst from us.

I sip cool water. It is measured
in and out of my kidneys in millilitres.

When the drain is removed
my wound makes a lake of the bed.

All about me is liquid.
The lines in my neck are tributaries

of amoxicillin, metronidazole,
parenteral nutrition – I cannot detach.

Salt lines my mouth
without passing my lips.

I vomit the colour of forests,
yet the floor is free of needles:

they lodge in my veins, reduce
my bloody portrait to a periodic table.

The phlebotomist knows I am phobic.
She says think of nice things.

Relief for Frank comes in bolus morphine.
He is silent when they move him.

On ward 3 Tom Selleck is outside in a pine tree,
John Lennon is invisible as oxygen.

This is what I have to look forward to.
No one tells me this.

Ariel Rising

Epileptic he says, darkening his prescription pad.
Like your mad Aunt Juana mouths Mum to Dad.
A fluke, my just-crawling hand finding the
sharpness of a shattered lightbulb, spasming at the
first sight of my own blood. The sharpness enters
me then, like a fragment from a sorcerer's mirror.
I am taboo, labelled, banned. A barbiturate junkie
before I can walk. My slothful blood, saturated.
Pocketing my tiny brown bottle of suicide, *Eat
me, Eat me.* But inside I'm a mayfly struggling
upwards, through this thick brown litany of *can't*
*** *Misdiagnosis* declares a young doctor four
decades later, unwriting my life. Two twitching years
to unknit the ravel in my blood and then like Ariel,
I'm unbound, blood light and pure as air.

At 21

I hauled your body alongside the carriages
of the Jubilee line and no one stopped to help.
I made a pact with your body to maul you
from the inside until coiled and whimpering
it rains rich blood from your arse.
The body that would sweep through dancefloors
of meat-market clubs and crush cigarettes
with slut-red heels. I'd watch you
how you girls would work your bodies
& dangle salted kebab meat into open mouths.
Now I will spread through your dancing-bones,
I'll make every vertebrae in that spine
slowly crumble and whine
and every needle-punch of pain
is worth it to laugh
when I fill your clothes
with warm shit.

Acute Care Ward C

The old lady calls the nurse a bitch
as she tries to prise her from the urine-stained
mattress. We all watch, our coarse sheets
sour with sweat, bleach clouding the smell
of fetid specimens rotting on toilet shelves.
We are no one.

I am obsessed with the drip-stand
that has been tethered to me;
hypnotised by the droplets chasing
each other into my desiccated vein.
I drag this mortality the length of the room
and wince at the screech of its wheel.

Chronic Obstructive Pulmonary Disease

3 a.m. and there are thousands of us awake, our lungs
an abacus of beads whose gummed yellow loyalty
refuses to be cast off in coughs, glutinous retches.

Next stop – steroid city: a moon-face, a wisp of air
for each nostril, a clutch of carers on minimum wage,
a moribund bed. At 3 a.m. we're fantastical as monks,

riot around the manuscript, conjure foresters with pipes
who tap us like birch trees, deliver us in runnels of pure
liquid pearl; we birth our heads through closed curtains,

apprehend the sky, read with infant, twenty-first century
eyes how oxygen, nitrogen, all the bound elements
collapse past and future to a singularity, a breathless

Aquinas silence; at 3 a.m. our chests open like Bibles
on a lectern, marginalia gold-leafed in the cortisoned
dark; we see the persistence of love, how light

bequeaths itself as measurement so we can watch
stars travel outward, every domed night a stretched
mouth's cry, *Look! I'm millions of miles further away.*

Advert

I should have sold my colon on the black market.

'Madam, I'm afraid we need to remove it.'

*'Well, okay, I will let you do that, doctor, but it's gonna cost you.
Do you know how much I could get for this baby on the street?'*

Turns out there isn't really a market for large intestines.
There's more of a demand
for organs people can't live without.
I haven't missed out on a lucrative business opportunity,
though I bet I could have used it to sharpen my sales skills.

For sale:
One large intestine
Used, one female owner
22 years old, still in working order
Ideal for water and vitamin absorption
Comes with 155cm of faeces storage
Extra cells included, no extra charge
Useful and decorative
£1500 ono

Eating Myself to Death

I have made many excuses – have stood in front of the mirror,
grabbed onto my handles and told myself lies. Big fat ones.
All those years of keeping myself on a knife edge – you'd think

I was mad if I told you I used to be slim. That I used to
stick my fingers right to the back of my throat, retch it all
back up again. I could tell you of the years I lived

through numbers – 300 calories, size 8, size 10, 23 inch waist.
It's all about control – the things you can do, or be, if only
you are thin. When you slough off the pounds, you ease

the scars. The pangs of hunger tell you to be proud –
for the first time you have power over yourself, you do not feel
quite so crap. You have shed who you once were, you

can start again, clean. After a decade of depravation, I found
my flip side. Found my appetite. Was not cured. Gorged my pain –
if I was fit to burst, then I was numb. I could tell you

of the years I lived through numbers – 5000 calories, size 24,
sertraline, 50mg, Prozac (too many), months spent in therapy, 38.
The doctor is worried – my blood sugar levels are too high, BMI

a disaster zone. I'm learning the risks of Type 2. I change
everything – all of the splurging on sweet chilli gone, whole
trifles with one spoon. I am a steamer of things, a chopper

of vegetables, stewer of healthy soups. I am wholewheat toast,
no butter. It's not about how you look – I cook to live as long
as I can, lay off the cakes, be here for my son. I could tell you

of the 46 years I lived before I learned that it's not about how
you appear. That it's not about big or small, curvy or straight,
up and down. Everything made from scratch, I aim for a menu

of simpler things, am lighter – I find that my legs are able to run.
It was never because I was big or small, nor connected to what I ate.
What happened was not my fault. In the end, it's all about shame.

Someone's Emotional Problem

Current Therapist is phoning Previous Therapist.

What if I am unmasked, accused
of changing my story in the retelling
of misrepresentation
of misunderstanding?

I clearly don't feel
the way I'm supposed to feel
but I can't seem to produce
whatever feeling I'm supposed to have.

I just want to work out
how to be a proper part of the human race
and Previous Therapist said it was

some kind of emotional problem

so I told Current Therapist that it is

some kind of emotional problem

but she didn't like that
and wouldn't say why
and wanted to check my records
so I certainly won't tell her
that I just want to die.

Shitting in a bag

In the beginning they provided
disposal sacks
with appliances.

Not, like a toaster with a free muffin rack
or grill pocket. More
single-use bags for life with a supply of bin liners.

When they seemed to cut back. Nobody asked
would you prefer to be dead?
I improvised. There are no consequences.

For dog waste you get black, sturdy, opaque.
Nappy carriers come in pastels,
see-through.

At the checkout in the corner shop
I'd incline towards someone waiting
outside with a lead

or back at the flat with a screaming baby. I have queued now
for eons, stomach coughing
nothing to see here.

I must have eaten too many peanuts.
There are no consequences
and I hear them:

Never even been pregnant.
Whit dug?
What is its name, exactly?

The shop assistant teen has an undigested mushroom slurping
down his right lens.
Where it falls, he catches it, on his palm.

I leave him a tenner tip.
Add another ten.
Exit rifling

sweetcorn pellets
from my concealed abdominal area.
Pitchuing. Pitchuing. Pitchuing.

Recognised items in bagging area.
Behind me they loot
hand sanitiser, loo roll and kitchen towel.

The man with the lead
is bent over his Labradoodle cooing
and scooping poop.

A lady with a pushchair is upturned by a Deliveroo rider.
Tins of lentils roll straight into drainage holes in the kerb.
She doesn't have a baby either.

Outpatient Appointment 11.40 a.m.

He leans deep over me; his breath, cool
as an anaesthetic, blankets my dread.
He does not speak. I sense his rule
of silence and my questions fade.

His warm palms touch my neck,
palpate my glands. His eyes,
half-closed, conceal what is at stake.
His hands draw down towards my thighs.

'May I?' His fingers check my groin.
Against my will my body starts to tense.
He moves away, leaves me alone,
the coldness of the couch is all I sense.

He's scribbling in a file. I'm in a chair.
He turns a page. I float my mind.
The unsaid saturates the air.
The pen is black. I watch his hand.

Vulnerable, adult

He can't put down his pint
without a beermat.

*– You're vulnerable – people must
take advantage. I want to
look after you.*

A slug of wine to tamp hackles;
don't overreact. But fight

instinct leaps my hand
from those thumb-strokes;
despite third date shoes,
flight flares.

– Why am I… vulnerable?
– Because you're…

Eyes dip to his empty palm,
fingers now caressing nothing.

Says he's no good with words,
just likes being out with a girl;
it's been a while.

– And you'll need me…
Still working my fingers' ghosts.

Fight melts like the teary fog
on his glass – can't touch
his dewiness,
even for one night.

I rip up both beermats,
then leave.

Trapped

half formed thoughts sentences stuck unwritten words unable to write words unable to spell words stuck mind stuck i am stuck here me or ME here or trapped words written trapped inside sentences fog want out words want me not ME want out want help i want to be able to write my honours thesis without getting stuck trying words get stuck inside me cant think no no no no stop. lie down. sleep. rest. rest. rest. resting and it doesnt get better still cant see words cant see write feel sorry bad day sorry tired sorry cant help sorry it sorry no sorry cant sorry want to die but sorry i am stuck sorry didnt do it sorry lying down sorry sleeping sorry want words not sorry want help not sorry want out im not sorry stuck here stuck being sorry cant get out cant get up stuck sorry tired thinking hurts sorry stuck hurts words hurt sorry im sorry dont want this sorry nothing helps stuck here forever always stuck always sorry help me stuck sorry dont want to think need to think need to finish want to help me finish this i want to be healthy again i want to want to want to think words that finish sentences that start and end its so hard its hard i get stuck its bad today im sorry help stuck lying here sorry stuck sorry stuck sorry repeating sorry i am here sorry dont want this sorry stuck in this with ME or me or help me anyone sorry im sorry its hard im sorry its late im stuck trapped bed traps me here held stuck help me no sorry nothing helps me cant think thoughts think anything i miss stuck miss me miss life miss everything miss writing dancing laughing walking skipping singing kissing standing talking wishing hoping. me.

Clammed Up

The girl who was tight as a clam was told
it was a 'condition'. It was made clear
to her that this wasn't as it should be.

She was told she needed prying open
with tools, small tools inserted,
then bigger, until she could perform
her purpose as a woman properly.

So, she leaned into billowing pillows,
breathed out frowns and doubts
and tried to fix the issue
between her soft white thighs. The nacre plastic
too foreign to become part of her.

Because as a woman, she is a vessel
to be filled by men – at their desire,
at their pleasure; not that hers didn't matter,
but it mattered less.

She thought about two women
coming together: no intercourse
is taking place, no sex
without a man. All that counts
is what's inside.

Oh hush – this embarrassment. The patriarchal
lens through which we view
everything becomes fogged
with her breath as the girl clenches
a fist and gives in.

Happy Birthday

Dear Charlie
Happy Birthday
Have a great day.
We look forward to seeing you in a few weeks.
We are both so proud of all you have achieved this year
    in spite of everything.
Glad the health problems are behind you.
All our Love,
Mum & Gordy

Dear Charlie
Happy Birthday
This year has been a tough one but we will all get
    to the bottom of this together.
All our Love,
Mum & Gordy

Dear Charlie,
Happy 25th Birthday.
We are so sorry that you are so unwell but let's hope
    you will soon get the diagnosis and
treatment you need and start to feel yourself again.
You have been very brave.
All our Love,
Mum & Gordy

Dear Charlie,
Happy Birthday.
We hope this year is easier than the last.
We will find you doctors who believe.
And find the money for an electric wheelchair.
If we could have your pain so that you didn't have
    to suffer we would.
All our Love,
Mum & Gordy

Dear Charlie,
Happy Birthday.
Persist.
All our Love,
Mum & Gordy

Checkup

She has few memories
untouched by these meetings,
these stiff seats and clotted magazines;
she is always the youngest
and is observed with interest
as she steps carefully over
the pale sea carpet which offers
little peace really,
for she thinks it is possibly deeper
underneath than she could stand.

Once she has counted three patients,
each one colourless,
six pallid hands in total,
she too is called from the waiting room
and brought into focus;
a man examines her violet eye
whilst she tries in earnest
to settle her breath
and steady her legs
underneath her chair.

When she is asked about pain
it becomes much harder
to face the doctor at all;
a small throb begins to boil
in the left hand side of her jaw
and she wonders if he can see
the water threatening to render him
awkward and soft
as it runs off her cheek
and onto his palm.

But she is saved by a knock:
an elderly woman has cut her hand
on a broken glass bottle
from her prescription bag,
so whilst the doctor goes out to take a look
she is left alone in his room
to touch the jag and tooth
of a silver letter knife
that if held right there against her face
might draw an ache that he could see.

But she doesn't do that;
too soon the doctor returns
with his crag tooth and grin,
a crimson fingerprint on his coat,
to sign over a list
of six new medicines
which she grips between her fingers
as she drifts back through the waiting room,
a little more sheer than before,
her toes just slipping below the pale sea.

Ehlers-Danlos Syndrome

When I say it's my neck –

I don't mean the pain.
That's the crowbar behind
my shoulder blade,
the vice my skull is gripped in.
The knitting needle
through my trapezius.
The slow ache that spreads
through my arms and legs.

I don't mean the immobility.
That's the elephant
slowness of my thighs,
the wet pasta limp
of lifting a bag.

I don't mean the fatigue.
That's the sinking-sand-tug
sucking at my limbs.
That's the heavy drapes
it's made of my eyelids.

I don't mean the stiffness.
That's my legs, which had
carried me up the Eiffel Tower,
had run across town,
had danced until 3 a.m.

When I say it's my neck –

I mean look – see:
it's twisted, it bends
a way it shouldn't.
It doesn't work,
I can show you.
You can see it, so
you might believe me.

Occupational Therapist

So… where to start? Hello. Well, the thing is –
these lungs are meat wings in a flap on steepening subway stairs.
At night they panic to work, even when it's shut
and, even though it's shut, the catering staff are there,
the Exec, students, their parents, the Vice Chancellor.
I am naked without a Powerpoint presentation, also my teeth have fallen out.
I drink coffee for hours, my face tight as a window,
and shovel the cold innards of Tupperware. It's not a dream!
When I wake, the Lovers card is ripped in shreds in my bed.

Don't get me wrong, it's not that I'm *in love* with my job.
It's more like assisting my lover seduce Tory ministers he fancies,
and powering the couple's electric candles
all night on a treadmill
so I can be trim because that's how he likes me,
meanwhile writing a lecture on Gramsci's concept of hegemony
before cleaning up their caviar smears
till I'm too knackered to canvas or picket or give a shit.

Sorry this is turning so confessional –
it's just that I've read that lungs are an instrument of voice
like 'an orator to a king' (Robert Burton, 1621)
but I can't locate my inner king

and the orator is managing her reputational yardstick.
Also, when I'm home I scrub the king's toilet.
Or maybe I am the king's toilet. Come to think of it,
there are several specific men
hunkered down on my chest even when I do sun salutations
and execute other vertical esoteric positions in the ozone of the underpass.

Do I smoke? Not so much now. Although I've loved the deep inhale
that catches at membranes and nerves before the outbreath;
that gateless gate to nothingness.
Yes, a walk-in chest X-ray. Yes, four weeks. Yes, gradual return.
Thanks for listening. I'll contact HR – they'll sort me out.

Beep

I have been dating an anaesthetist. But it isn't going as planned and I think I might end it. It's been three dates now and not once has he told me that, in his opinion, I've still got some of the general anaesthetic left in me from seven years ago and it's very rare but sometimes it can stay in you for that long and you don't always notice, it's just there, in you a little bit and it's okay because his friend is working late tonight and if we go now he'll be able to see me because it's a Thursday and his friend owes him a favour and his friend can do a quick assessment, just to make sure he's right, because these things do have to be done properly, but if he is right, after hanging out with me and looking at the black gunk in the corner of my eyes which is too much even accounting for the eyeliner, then his friend will put suction cups on my eyes and nose and ears and mouth and turn the machine on and I'll interrupt at that point and say sometimes my head does feel like a swelling and he'll reach for his car keys and carry on saying his friend, the doctor, will drain all the leftover anaesthetic and it will be all black and he'll put it in a big bag and put it in the bin and then clean my face off with a cold wet wipe and then I'm going to feel so awake.

Birth Trauma (PTSD)

The lump of rose quartz is deadly,
squatting on the mantle watching
everything. It swallows the light
from the lounge, unearthing the ring
where the birthing pool stood.

I kneel daily to scrub the stain
with warm water and vinegar,
the crystal towering above
my bowed head, crowing
triumphantly over pickled hands.

It jeers at me each morning
as I tiptoe past, seeking refuge
in the kitchen with the radio
and the silver coffee pot, the volume
turned right up to mask the cackling.

The red bird and her sisters

Get a lot of housebound nutters won't let me in because I'm wearing aftershave.

I've waited nine months to see this ME specialist. Thank god I'm not a house visit.

A student observing, young guy, beard-plait, breathing heavy beside me.

Doc's face is a baboon's bum, whiskey wafts from his chin

stubble exact russet of my Daisy's guinea pig.

Right. Let's take a look-see, he says.

A click of Baboon's fingers; there's the creak of a coffin lid.

This horrifying nurse appears – she's the weird one from… *Zoolander*, is it?

Old as the hills, warts – *honestly* – long hat; she's a bat shot from the cupboard

behind beardy-sidekick's back. (He's staring, gripping his A4 in both pink hands).

Nursey's uniform is mauve, pure 1940s; black little shoes, crinkled

fawn stockings. Lips are a neatly made bed.

Go strip down to your undies, she croak-says. Up on the couch. Bend over.

And lean into the wall.

Hang your feet over the edge, Baboon grunts, taps the back of my heels.
A fleck of his spittle in the pool of my lower back.
Perfect... No sign of thyroid disease. Go slip your clothes back on, please.

I stripped off for *that*. Charlatan-perv, nightmare-nurse, student chap.

Dragging on my jeans, a label waves, a tiny white flag. That's all I need, knickers on inside-out this morning.

Baboon dusts his hands – so very *Now aren't I the accomplished man.*
Please sit. Yes. I think you have ME, he says.

I've known that for two years.
Baboon to young plait-beard: Daniel, sit.
Daniel sits, blushing.
Now, says Baboon, as if Here is the business, and Here is the getting down to it.

Do you have a third nipple?

No! What –

Are you sure? It's incredibly common. People don't realise they've got one –
or often more – 2, 3, even 4 – no bigger than a raisin… I'm conducting a study on
Supernumerary Nipples…'.

Photo of his wife-woman, desk-furnishing-smile. Christ.

How many ill women, demi-living? How many bend for him in their underwear?

My poor suffering sisters locking doors against his *aftershave*,
the least offensive thing about this visiting-dick-primate.

I wish an eruption of surplus nipples upon you and your frost-coffin nurse.

May they breed, chafe, turn to great oozing sores – here now old crook I communicate
my curse.

Today, I found the strength to be truly appalled by you.

Today I cared slightly, that I had my not-best-underwear on wrong.

*I even wondered if my arse had grown. Hell, I've been dead-alive, I don't care if my
behind's run riot! Let dear flesh spill over every waistband in the land!*

Today a red bird rose from my chest.

The strength to give a fig is the first sign of healing.

Telling the world about your methods, Doc, is the next.

54

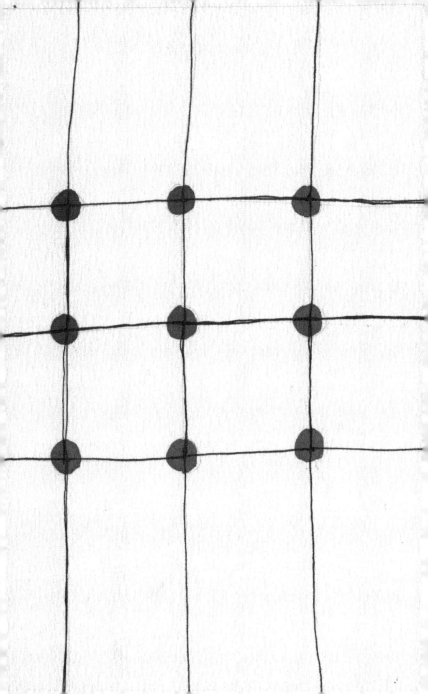

Snow

Snow
and the farmers
struggle to reach their cattle.
I watch on the news
as tractors
and men with snow up to the
top of their wellies
spend hours,
shovelling, ploughing,
keeping the animals alive.

Snow
at home in the suburbs,
I see children
with bright-coloured sledges
grinning, as they skate
down the hill,
on the road outside my home.
The children are warm in stripy woollen knits.

I pull the blanket over my knees.
I can't afford the extra heating.
As if making a trek across the tundra
I struggle to reach the kitchen.
Holding onto the three-wheeled walker,

I inch forward.
This is the last tea bag.
The milk has gone lumpy.
Congealing in the mug
which slips through my arthritic hands.
I watch it splinter around my feet.
I cry out.
I hear my agonised moan echo.

As I fall I strain to hear the TV.
Lying on the hard-tiled floor
I feel warmed by my own
sweet and hot urine.
I will grow cold and stale
as the night wears on.

Behind the evergreen hedges
and down the winding drives
my neighbours will be settling down.
An aperitif,
napkins on their knees,
music or a film?

I wonder whether the farmer
reached his cattle
in this snow.

It's good to talk
(a polite reminder)

It's good to talk,
and to help you do so
we have carefully curated
a list of acceptable talking points.
Please keep to this list
at all times.
Please do not discuss
situations that you find hard;
we do not need your negativity.
Do not talk about things we
might have got wrong.
This can be construed as
hurtful finger-pointing.
Do not tell us the scary parts.
They make us uncomfortable
and we do not like to be
uncomfortable.
We encourage you to
stay vague and positive.
When life is difficult
please remember to learn
a valuable lesson.

It is acceptable to mention anxiety
as long as you use a witty anecdote
or wry conversational tone.
Do not mention the visions
or the time you thought your family
was dead and you were reliving
your past in virtual reality.
This is too far.
People don't need to hear it.
Save it for your therapist.
In return for your kind acceptance
of these polite suggestions
we will endeavour to respond
to your 'talk' with virtual hugs,
photos of sunsets on beaches,
motivational quotes, and reminders
that all you need to do is ask for help,
providing you ask in the correct format
and for the correct help.
(Please see 'Just Ask For Help'
for further guidance.)

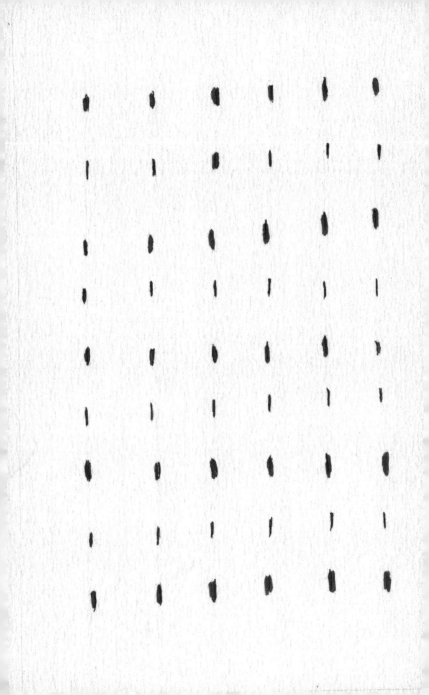

ACKNOWLEDGEMENTS

'Binge' by Sharon Black was first published in *Envoi*, issue 155, and subsequently in the collection *To Know Bedrock* (Pindrop, 2011).

'The Problem with Good Looking Oncologists' by Sharon Black was first published in *The Interpreters House*, issue 61.

'Cones' by Louisa Campbell was first published in *Under the Radar* in Autumn 2018, as a result of winning the Institute of Psychoanalysis Prize for Mental Health Workers and Trainees that year.

'Cross-Section with Contrast' by Stephanie Conn was first published in *Coast to Coast to Coast*.

'Outpatient Appointment 11.40 a.m.' by Marian Fielding was first published in *The Hippocrates Prize Anthology 2015*.

'High Dependency Unit' by Gillian Mellor was first published in the literary journal *Laldy!* and won third prize in the 2018 Clochoderick Press Poetry Competition.

ABOUT THE EDITORS

Amy Mackelden lives with MS, anxiety, and PCOS. She's the weekend editor at *Harper's BAZAAR*, and co-founded *Butcher's Dog* poetry magazine. In 2019, she was awarded a Developing Your Creative Practice grant from Arts Council England to undertake a short course in Narrative Medicine at Columbia University.

Dr Dylan Jaggard has a PhD in Philosophy from Birkbeck College, London, and has published work on aesthetics and ethics. He's lived with depression for most of his life.

ABOUT THE POETS

Cassandra Atherton is a widely anthologised Australian prose poet. She has written eight books of prose poetry and has recently been awarded Australia Council Grants to write a book of prose poetry on the atomic bomb. She is commissioning poeetry editor for *Westerly Magazine*.

Sharon Black is from Glasgow and lives in France. In 2019 she won The Guernsey International Poetry Competition and the London Magazine Poetry Prize. Her two collections are *To Know Bedrock* (Pindrop, 2011) and *The Art of Egg* (Pindrop, 2019), and her third, *The Last Woman Born on the Island*, is forthcoming from TLM Editions.

Astra Bloom won the Bare Fiction Prize for Poetry in 2015, came second in the Brighton story prize, won the Sussex flash fiction prize, and has been shortlisted by Bridport, Mslexia, and the 2019 London Magazine Essay Prize. She has writing in *Common People*, an anthology of working class writing edited by Kit de Waal.

Samara Bolton studies Creative Writing at the University of Chichester. In 2018 she was commended in the Foyle Young Poets of the Year Awards. Her ultimate goal is to highlight the positives that stem from darker times, extending the joy and catharsis of poetry to a broader audience.

Constance Bourg lives in the Flemish part of Belgium, where she volunteers at her local library and social food market. Her work has appeared or is forthcoming in *Frogpond*, *Haibun Today* and the Plath Poetry Project. She always says that she lives a 'part-time life' because of a chronic illness called ME/CFS.

Rachel Bower is the author of *Moon Milk* (Valley Press) and *Epistolarity and World Literature* (Palgrave Macmillan). Her poems and stories have been published in *Magma, Stand* and *New Welsh Reader,* and shortlisted for the London Magazine Poetry Prize and the White Review Short Story Prize.

Emily Brenchi is a 28-year-old writer, actor and disability rights activist. She has BA in English and Drama in 2012 from the University of Greenwich and has poetry published in Disability journal *Wordgathering.* She currently lives near Oxford and, as a sufferer of Crohn's Disease, is interested in exploring ideas around disability and the body on the page.

Sue Burge is freelance creative writing and film studies tutor based in North Norfolk. *Lumière,* her debut pamphlet, and *In the Kingdom of Shadows,* her first collection, were both published in 2018. Sue's second pamphlet, *The Saltwater Diaries,* will be published in Autumn 2020. www.sueburge.uk

Jane Burn lives in the North East of England. Her poems are widely published in many magazines and anthologies, have been nominated for The Forward and Pushcart Prize and have been placed in many poetry competitions.

Louisa Campbell used to be a registered mental health nurse and has complex PTSD and bipolar disorder. She has written about these experiences in her poetry pamphlets *The Happy Bus* (Picaroon Poetry, 2017) and *The Ward* (Paper Swans Press, 2018). She lives in Kent.

Stephanie Conn is a poet and PhD candidate from Northern Ireland. Her poetry collections *The Woman on the Other Side* (2016) and *Island* (2018) are published by

Doire Press. Her pamphlet *Copeland's Daughter* (2016) was published by Smith/Doorstep. Stephanie has Fibromyalgia and is currently researching Poetry and Chronic Illness.

Marc Darnell is a custodian in Papillion, Nebraska, and received his MFA from the University of Iowa. He has published poems in *The Lyric, Shot Glass Journal, Ragazine, Jam & Sand* and *The Literary Nest,* among others, and has forthcoming poems in *Fine Lines, The Pangolin Review,* and *POETiCA REVIEW.*

Marian Fielding's poem was inspired by the many tedious/terrifying times she has attended hospital in- and out-patient appointments. She has been published in *Orbis, South, South Bank Poetry* and *The Interpreter's House.* She was commended in The Hippocrates Prize Competition 2015. She is also a published short story writer.

Charlie Fitz is a sick and disabled artist, writer and poet living in Birmingham. Her work broadly explores experiences of illness whilst aiming to resist expectations that the 'sick' be patient or passive to medical paternalism. Find out more about her work at www.sickofbeingpatient.com.

Lucy Fox is a queer and disabled writer of poetry, prose, and all that lives in-between. She holds a BCA (Honours) in Creative Writing and owns more pairs of pyjamas than you. You will most often find her in bed, but you can also find her in *Imprint Magazine, Baby Teeth Arts Journal,* or on Twitter @LucyFox96.

Helena Goddard started writing poetry in 2006, so could be classed as a young poet as long as you don't find her birth certificate. She's had success in competitions, including the Plough International Poetry Prize and Poetry on the Lake.

She's been published in anthologies, *The Interpreter's House*, and the *Rialto*.

Rhiannon Grant lives in Birmingham. Her best work arises from personal experience, of spirituality as well as illness and the rest of life. As well as poetry, she writes LGBTQ+ novels and about religion. Her latest book, *Quakers Do What! Why?*, was published by Christian Alternative Books in 2020.

Paula Harris lives in New Zealand, where she writes and sleeps a lot, because that's what depression makes you do. She won the 2018 Janet B. McCabe Poetry Prize and her work has been in Queen Mob's Teahouse, Kissing Dynamite, Barren, SWWIM, Glass and others. Find her on Twitter @paulaoffkilter or on her website, www.paulaharris.co.nz

Holly Magill has had poetry in numerous magazines and anthologies. She is co-editor at *Atrium* (www.atriumpoetry. com). Her first pamphlet, *The Becoming of Lady Flambé*, is available from Indigo Dreams Publishing.

Gillian Mellor lives near Moffat in Scotland and has the good fortune to co-own The Moffat Bookshop and to have been published in *Poetry Scotland, The Dangerous Women Project* and to have won The Biggar Science Festival Writing Competition in 2019.

Ruth Middleton, a proud Yorkshire woman, is passionate about diversity and inclusion. With a background in mental health, she writes for her own wellbeing. Disability and illness followed a life changing accident in 2000. Ruth continues to enjoy travelling, politics, literature, friends, tennis and the Dales. She is very fond of sheep!

Rebekah Miron is a Creative Writing graduate from the University of Cambridge. Her poetry has been published in various journals both in print and online. In 2020, she was shortlisted for the Frogmore Poetry Prize and the Sweet Lit Poetry Contest. She suffers from hemiplegic migraine disorder and currently lives in Zurich, Switzerland.

Jess Redway studied Literature and Contemporary Popular Knowledges in Lincoln and Winchester. She is now training to be a mental health nurse in Hampshire. Sometimes she passes the time writing poems or sewing quilts. She may not be as entirely wholesome as this makes her sound.

Hollie Richards is a researcher from Bristol, although she spent most of her childhood living on a Hebridean island. She was longlisted for the Penguin Random House Write Now Program in 2017 and has had a number of poems published in anthologies. She likes puffins and Welsh coastal paths.

Sam Rose is a writer from Northamptonshire and the editor of *Peeking Cat Poetry Magazine*. She is a three times cancer survivor and a PhD student, researching the role of poetry in psycho-oncology. She has had work published in over 50 venues. Find her at https://www.writersam.co.uk and on Twitter @writersamr.

Mollie Russell cannot be stopped by silver bullets or religious iconography. Instead, she delivers conversational confessions about autism, depression, and some really terrible birthday parties. She graduated from the University of Winchester with a first-class degree in Creative Writing and English Literature and currently lives in South Wales.

Jane Salmons is from Stourbridge in the Black Country. She has an MA in Creative Writing from the Open University and has been published in journals and webzines including *Poetry Salzburg Review, Ink, Sweat and Tears* and *The Ekphrastic Review*, among others.

Helen Seymour is a spoken-word-artist-human-poet-performance-person. She likes pretending to be a bear and is also a bit obsessed with death but in quite a charming way. If she wasn't a spoken-word-artist-human-poet-performance-person she thinks she'd be a pharmacist from the past. Find her on Instagram: @whathelens

Mairi-Claire Traynor is an Edinburgh based poet who grew up in Ayrshire. She is fascinated by fleeting moments and makes sense of the world through her writing. In 2019 Mairi-Claire was long listed for Nine Arches Primers. Mairi-Claire is a survivor of childhood leukaemia and of Crohn's disease in adulthood.

Alison Winch's pamphlet *Trouble* was published by The Emma Press in 2016. Her debut collection is *Darling, It's Me* (Penned in the Margins 2019).

ABOUT THE EMMA PRESS

small press, big dreams

☙❧

The Emma Press is an independent publisher dedicated to producing beautiful, thought-provoking books. It was founded in 2012 by Emma Dai'an Wright in Winnersh and is now based in the Jewellery Quarter in Birmingham, UK.

The Emma Press publishes themed poetry anthologies, single-author poetry and fiction chapbooks and books for children, with a growing list of translations. It was awarded funding from Arts Council England in 2020 through the Elevate programme, for diverse-led arts organisations to build resilience.

The Emma Press has been shortlisted for the Michael Marks Award for Poetry Pamphlet Publishers in 2014, 2015, 2016 and 2018, winning in 2016.

The Emma Press is passionate about publishing literature which is welcoming and accessible. Sign up to the Emma Press newsletter to hear about upcoming events, publications and calls for submissions.

theemmapress.com

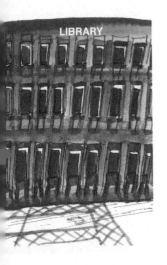

EVERYTHING THAT CAN HAPPEN
POEMS ABOUT THE FUTURE
Edited by Suzannah Evans & Tom Sastry
RRP £10 / ISBN 978-1-910139-52-3

The poems in this anthology explore time, language, changing landscapes, future selves, uncertainty, catastrophe and civilisation. Whether imagining a distant, apocalyptic future or the moment we live in, nudged slightly beyond what we know, the poems ask what we can do to prepare ourselves for a future that edges a little closer every day.

THE EMMA PRESS ANTHOLOGY
OF CONTEMPORARY GOTHIC VERSE
Edited by Nisha Bhakoo
RRP £10 / ISBN 978-1-912915-36-1

The Emma Press Anthology of Contemporary Gothic Verse is haunting, romantic, and full of dark doorways and strange spaces which readers will get thoroughly lost in. It's a hand in a velvet glove, ready to grasp you by the elbow and lead you through an array of ravishing and heart-racing encounters.

In Transit: Poems of Travel
Edited by Sarah Jackson & Tim Youngs
RRP £10 / ISBN 978-1-910139-94-3

Travelling from one place to another is never as simple as getting from A to B. Whether you're sailing in a stately cruise liner or running for a grimy commuter train, your mode of transport affects the way you look at the things around you. The poems in this anthology look at the ways in which travelling can change us, whether we enjoy or endure it.

Some Cannot Be Caught: The Emma Press Book of Beasts
Edited by Anja Konig & Liane Strauss
RRP £10 / ISBN 978-1-910139-88-2

This anthology rustles and roars with the voices of animals and humans, co-existing on Earth with varying degrees of harmony. A scorpion appears in a shower; a deer jumps in front of a car. A swarm of snowfleas seethes through leaf litter; children bait a gorilla at the zoo. The poems in this anthology examine hierarchy, herds, power, and the price we pay for belonging.